Michelle Gussow:
Tales From the E-List

MICHELLE GUSSOW

authorHOUSE®

For Kathy Garver who, no matter what I told her I want to do, always simply said, "You should."

AuthorHouse™
1663 Liberty Drive
Bloomington, IN 47403
www.authorhouse.com
Phone: 1 (800) 839-8640

Published by AuthorHouse 09/24/2019

ISBN: 978-1-7283-2897-3 (sc)
ISBN: 978-1-7283-2898-0 (e)

Print information available on the last page.

Any people depicted in stock imagery provided by Getty Images are models, and such images are being used for illustrative purposes only. Certain stock imagery © Getty Images.

This book is printed on acid-free paper.

Contents

Foreword

I've written books, written and directed independent film, acted in independent film and TV. done story telling, hosted and performed in live shows and at age 55 decided to be a pin-up girl. Passion for this has engulfed every cell in my body. I have shared many of the stories in this book with many people over the years. Those times were often met with a, "You know, you should write a book." Written the way I would share these stories with friends or even an audience, I hope they inject at least a little bit of humor into your day. And, I hope you enjoy some of the highlights from my decades on the E- list.

Genesis of the Entertainment Bug

I do not know specifically when I first decided that I wanted to be on TV. In general it happened when I was around four-years-old while I was watching the "Popeye and Janie" show, a local cartoon program that aired in the afternoons on WTTV channel four. The show consisted of a host named Janie who introduced cartoons from her treehouse. At some point I made up my mind that that was what I wanted to do when I grew up. And I did not simply continue to watch the show and say to myself that it was what I was going to do. Indeed, I started practicing. I spent an undocumented amount of time in my bedroom sitting on my bed, practicing introducing cartoons using the mirror on my dresser as the television camera. I worked at being cheerful and upbeat when I introduced them and made sure I was smiling just the way Janie did.

I had become a pretty good at cartoon introduction when Janie left her treehouse to have a baby. The replacement show, no longer from the treehouse was called "Sally Jo and Friends" Sally Jo hosted the show with her big friendly sheepdog. She introduced cartoons pretty much the same as Janie had so I found nothing new to learn... about introducing cartoons anyway. Sally Jo did something Janie never had. While Janie did have Brownie Troops and the like visit her treehouse they always just sat there. Sally Jo lined them up and introduced WTTV viewers to roll call.

Yes, roll call, a line of nervous kids trying to remember their names, ages and whoever their parents had told them to say "hi" to. Sally Jo would stoop to their level, stick a microphone in their faces and ask, "What's your name?" I will never forget that more that one child over the years held up two fingers and responded, "Three." They were obviously prepared for the second part of the interview. It is still a running joke in our house.

Naturally, I needed to practice this aspect of hosting a cartoon show. For this I commandeered the services of my younger sister. The poor girl had to be every child in the roll call line. While I got experienced in interviewing children as to their names and ages my sister developed quite a knack for inventing names, giving an age for the name and even making it interesting by adding a, "Hi, grandma. Hi, Aunt

Mary." This "rehearsal" actually paid off for her before it did me as several years later her Brownie Troop went on "Debbie's Place," the show that replaced "Sally Jo and Friends." Needless to say she was well prepared for the roll call.

As an aside, Debbie was not the last in the lineup. Debbie moved and Peggy came in with "Peggy's World". Then at some point the show got cut from one hour to half an hour and renamed "Popeye and Peggy"... guess you could say full circle. Some time years before, Janie had returned but was on in the mornings. That outlasted the afternoon show. Also for years we had "Cowboy Bob's Chuckwagon Theater." He ended up with a half an hour in the morning before Janie with "Cowboy Bob's Corral". At some point all the cartoon shows vanished from the lineup, so my plans to have "Michelle's Universe" or whatever they would have called it fell by the wayside.

Lucky thing I had practiced for more than just the possibility of hosting the kids' cartoon show.

Another show watched regularly in our house and in homes across the WLWT viewing area was "The Paul Dixon Show." Every morning Bonnie Lou and Colleen Sharp came out in front of a live studio audience and with "Elvis is in the building, Beatlemania" type enthusiasm would announce to

those in the studio and those viewing at home, "Here he is...
the one, the only...Paul Baby!"

Paul Dixon would come out, ask everyone where they were
all from. Everyone in the audience would shout an answer at
the same time. Then Paul Baby would say that it had to be
the youngest, most attractive group of women they've ever
had in the audience. The show was entertaining for its time.
It brought us knee ticklers and kanee knockers. Most of all
it was commercial free... okay, not exactly. Paul, Bonnie Lou
and Colleen talked about the products during the show. This,
too, was something to which I could aspire.

So when I wasn't practicing introducing cartoons I was in
front of my mirror talking about products. I would hold up
the tissue box from my room and talk about how it was the
softest brand of tissue. If I had a snack I would talk about
how it was the best tasting whatever it was. I also rehearsed
my own version of the Paul Baby introduction.

At this point I actually started to take note of any show that
involved someone introducing someone or something. For
quite some time I was ready, willing and able to take over
for Cathy Baker, who with a high-pitched voice and flip of
her hair let audiences know every week, "Now here's Buck

and Roy with ‚Pickin' and Grinnin'!" I could cheerfully say, "That's all!" with the best of them. Never got that little hair flip down, though. But even so I was a natural and nothing could stop me.

In the Beginning There Were Dreadful School Programs

Even though I was practicing to introduce cartoons and talk about everthing from snack foods to soap, my first actual experience with performing came in the form that it does for so many... school plays/pageants. I am sure many of your favorite actors and actresses have a story to tell about playing a tomato in the play about the four food groups or some equally demanding role. For me it was preschool and the three classes joined to put on a circus. My first role was also to be my first disappointing role. I had wanted to be the tightrope walker. (She didn't have to walk a real tightrope, just a straight line on the gymnasium floor.) Or I wanted to be one of the girls who was supposed to gallop in a circle like she was riding a beautiful white horse. But, alas, these parts were given to cute little blonde girls in the class. I, on the other hand, was assigned to be one of five penguins. They had head-to-toe penguin costumes for us and we were to waddle to the center of the ring and back while singing a lively little tune called, "Peter, Peter Penguin." (If you are curious you can hear this song on youtube, not performed by me.). I don't know if I realized at the time that penguins were not part of a real-life circus.

The next stand-out opportunity was when I attended day camp in the summer following second grade. The day camp was structured like school in that one day a week we had music, one art and one drama. When it was time for our group to do its play we did get to have more drama days so we could rehearse. The play that was chosen for us to do was about the biblical prophet Deborah and how she helped defeat Cicero's army. The camp paired us with the boys' group of the same grade and the drama counselor made sure that everyone got to do something.

It was this play that gave me my "Hark! Who goes there?" moment. Most people remember the episode of "The Brady Bunch" where Marcia is cast in the school play as Juliet. In the episode, Peter and Jan are very excited because they have been cast as palace guards. Peter's line was "Hark!" and Jan said, "Who goes there?"

Well, in that spirit I was cast as one of Deborah's daughters. There is a scene where she and the other daughter run in. My stage sister yells, "Mommy, mommy." And I say excitedly, "Boaz is here!" For the record I remember the names of the other kids who had the roles and am even friends with some of them on social media.

And speaking of Bible stories... Sunday School was another great candidate for stage experience. And what fun that was. Our class did a play about Masada, complete with the discussion and decision to commit suicide. I was around ten-years-old at the time.(and people wonder why I was so messed up.) One year we also did a play about the Mogen David Adom which is the Israeli Red Cross. I think the teacher that year wanted to be a cheerleader because she had us start out the play by cheer spelling Mogen David Adom. Give me an "M!" Of course, by the time we were done spelling it out the play was halfway over.

I did not find these shows particularly enjoyable. I do not even think that at the time I counted them as real acting. It was just school. It was just another assignment to be completed. And often, as with any other assignment we were given a grade for the performance and subsequently tested on the material.

Two things came from this. One, my desire to do some "real" performing grew. And two. my family's hopes that these school plays would "get it out of my system" were dashed.

02134

So, how many of you found yourselves singing the number that is the title of this tale? If you are someone who did, or now that I've mentioned it, you find yourself singing it now, you grew up watching a show on PBS called "Zoom." My memories of it are actually very hazy but its very existence put the idea in my head that I did not have to wait until I grew up to be on televsion. Of course, I saw kids on TV all the time but those kids seemed to be far away in some far-off, distant land that I would never get to visit. I guess because "Zoom" was on PBS I got the idea that someone, somewhere was doing local programming with people my age.

So this was also the point at which my parents went out of their way to discourage me. This even included lying to me by telling me that the local shows were not really done locally. It hit me rather hard when a classmate of mine made commericals for the Pacer Pals and Country Line Cheese, My mother still tried to insist they had been filmed elsewhere.

I heard countless times how it was a pipe dream, that I would never make it in that business, that I shouldn't waste time on it. If someone else tried to encourage me they were told not to encourage me. My grandmother even started saying, "Oh, you don't want to do that."

They also questioned why it wasn't enough for me to just do the little plays at school and in camp. They suggested I should just try to find something else to like doing. I would occasionally ask, "Like what." I don't think they had any real recommendations because it would be suggested that I read a book or go play outside. Yes, I am aware that it made no sense. Nor could they understand why I didn't want to put as much energy into something I didn't want to do. They pondered on why it wasn't out of my system yet. And I'd hear them bemoan, "She *has* to grow out of it eventually."

But I wanted to be an actor... so I played along. I got them to believe I had found another life goal. To do this, though, I started speaking in incomplete sentences. I would say, "I want to be a teacher." That made everyone happy. The rest of the sentence that remained unspoken was, "On television, like Karen Valentine." I remember in fifth and sixth grade it was, "I want to be a cop." The rest of that sentence was, "On television, like Peggy Lipton on ,The Mod Squad."

By the way, for any of you who watched "The Mod Squad" you may remember how when the episode was wrapping up and the music would start to swell and the cast members were walking away or whatever, there would be a freeze frame. This was the first show I saw do this. I wasn't sure how it was done but when I practiced to play a cop on TV I actually practiced "freezing." It was just getting deeper in my system.

Getting a Real Taste

Student film in Indiana in the 1970s was an entirely different species than one sees as the student film industry of today. For one it was literally just a class... and a throwaway class at that. They were assigned various projects with a number of constraints, criteria, etc... decided by the teacher. The films were graded, never viewed, even by the class in most cases and then became property of the school. (This is via the "filmmakers" at the time.) They were not actually student filmmakers but rather students simply taking a film class. Looking back I would have called it "Home Movies 101."

I first became involved with Home Movies 101 when I was twelve-years-old through the brother of my writing mentor who attended school with people who took this class. The students all needed people to "act" in their projects and the brother thought of me. And having up until then given all my time to the stage I was ready to branch out.

Let us explore these extraordinary cinematic masterpieces. Too sarcastic?

Two Men Too

Set on a floor of a high rise apartment building this movie followed the happenings of the occupants of three of the apartments, through the eyes and mouth of the fourth, a busybody, Gladys Kravitz type who spent her days observing and listening then reporting her view of what happened to her sister later that night. Her first report which was on her move-in day involved her telling her sister who lived in the other units. She reports of the young couple with the baby, the teenager (me) who seems to have no parents and "We have, two men too."

I only know this because I was on the set when it was filmed. I have no idea what the entire thing looked like completed, never even had any part of the script for a scene in which I was not.

Now even though this was essentially a general audience movie, I played the daughter of a prostitute who did indeed spend the majority of the time fending for herself. Part of the assignment was that the movie had to include a musical number. The scene called for me to be cleaning the kitchen and singing along with "The House of the Rising Sun" that was playing on the radio. so this became not only my first student film but the first musical performance since "Peter, Peter Penguin."

A Little Something for the Police Department

Filmed after "Two Men Too" but I heard that it had been finished first, I affectionately refer to working on this movie as "The Days of Fake Nails and Fake Tan."

This movie involved two street gangs and the young, neighborhood social worker tasked with keeping them from killing each other. This particular assignment had to include a "surprise ending" and my character Tina was supposed to be just that. They apparently speak of waiting on her to get to the scene where two gangs are ready to go at it but the police have arrived in anticipation of the rumble. Everyone is now on edge waiting for the mysterious Tina to arrive to defuse the situation. The character of Tina was actually about twenty or so-years old and a latina to boot, but I was the only female available. Luckily I was well... well-developed even at my young age and they had access to all the cheap makeup they could get their hands on.

They hauled me off for an extensive makeup job which included a nasty product you might remember called "Sudden

Tan" to make it look like I had darker skin. Problem for me was it took on an orange tinge rather than giving me the appearance of a tan and it went on unevenly and looked blotchy. They plopped a wig on my head that looked like something out of the musical "Hairspray," stuck missized fake nails on my hands and said I was ready to go. (I think if anyone even saw this today they would never know it was me. I didn't know it was me when I looked in the mirror.)

All I was required to do for this movie was emerge from a taxicab and be shot down by an unscrupulous detective. While I am on the ground he is supposed to kick my dead body. This guy was not an actor, just someone related to the producer. And he really kicked me...hard. They had to get it in one take so maybe this was my best acting performance ever as I remained motionless. I also gave a pretty good performance the next few days in school trying to not act embarrassed with the layers of fake tan. The product never came off as easily as it went on.

Banks of the Ohio

So this student had the idea to tell the story of a song through video. There is a song called "Banks of the Ohio" which by chance happened to be on an Olivia Newton-John album I had. I was originally cast to be the person singing the song over the film. The song deals with a mariticide which happens down by the banks of the Ohio. Yes, took me back to my days in the Masada play. The actress cast in the role was literally a no-show. Gee, who could turn down all the money and fame? So they did the makeup bit again to make me look older and sent me in front of the camera to slay my lover who would not marry me.

And so ended that semester.

I would not do another student project until a few years later. It seemed the school was now offering Home Movies 201 because I was approached by one of the students from a few years prior.

Downtown

In this film which he called the sequel to "Two Men Too" (everyone was just waiting with bated breath for that one), I revamped my role as the daughter of the prostitute who was now grown and ran her own brothel. It was another "surprise ending" type thing as no one was supposed to know who I was. I was put in a big blonde wig, five layers of makeup and my favorite fake nails. My wardrobe was a full satin dressing gown. If you want to envision it, think Tammy Faye Baker with a Dolly Parton wig dressed like Mrs. Roper from "Three's Company." She eventually becomes an evangelist and there is this big reveal where I take off the wig and false eyelashes and – whoa- it's what's her name from "Two Men Too."

It would be two years until the next student project.

Decade of the Rebel Rouser

Set over the decade of the 1960s, this project followed Kris Barkley who was a teen prodigy having received her doctorate in political science at age fourteen. Both political parties wanted her on board and she finds herself attached to the democrats with the victory of John F. Kennedy. With the death of Robert F. Kennedy in 1968, she finds herself aligned with the republicans and abandoning the scene altogether in the wake of Kent State. This film offered me my first and only stint in a body suit for a scene in a bubblebath. The producer told me he would double my salary for doing that scene. (Think: twice nothing is...?)

The Next Decade

Same student filmmaker, the following year, different decade, this sequel to "Decade of the Rebel Rouser" followed Kris in her new life as an entertainment promotor with a continuous barrage of political personalities attempting to sway her back into the fold. This was made the following year during which time I was attending the university that offered the class. This led to what came to be the only student film during this time period that I ever actually got to see.

Runner Astray

In a project to which I always referred as "The Jazz Singer, Lite" Truly Oswald has just won the fictional Global Sweepstakes. Her win brings out long-lost friends and relatives all claiming to be in dire straits. Fed up, she and her best friend Donna take to the road in a motor home in search of people who are truly needy. Along the way they meet Doug who has escaped his life where his parents are expecting him to become a rabbi. And wackiness ensues in this project whose requirements were a life-altering event and two musical numbers. The big number takes place in a gypsy camp with me giving a grand performance of "Those Were the Days" accompanied by an accordion.

For some reason it was decided that two or three of the completed projects that semester would be screened by the class and their guests. They did it big with a red carpet party immediately following. The evening provided me two times that I was left completely dumbfounded. The first occurred when the big number in the gypsy camp ended and the class broke into applause. The second happened when I had my "entrance" on the carpet into the party room and was greeted by another round of applause. I really was taken aback as sitting in the screening all I could think is that the movie was a real ,turkey.' But it was my first taste of a "real" ovation. And as everyone continued to hope, it still was not "out of my system."

As an aside, I was recognized several years later for this film. This story is included in the "Bonus" section of this book.

Another Minor Taste

I do have to mention another stellar film in which I appeared somewhere in the summer between my freshman and sophomore years of high school. There was a local photography club that thought it would be fun to expand to making home movies. They had been toying with movie cameras for some time before the club president had this brilliant idea to have a club contest. In this case, I was approached through a friend's father's friend. He had this great concept to spoof those old Frankie and Annette beach movies. Now I personally never saw a script or was told a plot, but what was needed from me was apparently very important to the spoof.

There is a scene in the classic Frankie and Annette movie "Beach Blanket Bingo" where everyone is gathered in the beach house and there is a guy playing an acoustic guitar. He strums an intro and says, "Go, Donna!" At that, Donna Loren who is sitting on the hearth roasting a hotdog belts out a song called, "It Only Hurts When I Cry." This was what the club member wanted/needed. They came to my house one afternoon; the film maker and an acoustic guitar player. I was filmed singing "It Only Hurts When I Cry" while sitting on our fireplace hearth. I was thanked profusely, paid ten dollars and like my student film experiences never did see the final project. Heck, I don't even know if that guy won the prize.

Just a little point of interest. More recently, thanks to the wonders of social media I got the opportunity to share this with Donna Loren.

A Wink and a Nod to Indie Film

I imagine enough time has passed that most people were either not born yet or have simply forgotten that using the term "indie film" was synonymous with saying, "adult film". Okay, maybe not synonymous. More along the lines of "It's an ‚independent film (wink, wink.)"

For the record I was asked to do a few "independent films of the "wink, wink" variety. One sleazebag even used the old, "I'll make you a star" line. I was not in that big of a hurry to be famous... okay, maybe I was in that big of a hurry but not taking *that* particular route.

For all intents and purposes for this story I am not considering the student film experience of yore as independent film when I say I did one... or rather was cast in one indie film in the mid 1980s. It was not, I repeat, not of the "indie, wink, wink" variety.

It was the mid 1980s and I heard from a friend of a friend of an acquaintance that a friend of theirs was making a mockumentary type film based on a Mamas and Papas type group. This friend thought that I would be ideal for the Mama Cass character. I submitted photos and participated in a singing audition and like I mentioned was cast in the role. The producer seemed very excited about the project and had a continued mantra during the few weeks of this process. It involved the facts that he was writing original songs for the project and that he had signed the actor who played Mario on "Joanie Loves Chachi" to play the Papa John character.

For a three week period I, along with two other actors got together with the producer to rehearse. This mostly involved becoming the characters and learning to ad-lib as them. I remember us asking ourselves exactly when it was we were going to rehearse with Mario from "Joanie Loves Chachi."

At the beginning of week four, I got a call from one of the other cast members asking if I had heard anything from the producer about the next rehearsal. He said that he had attempted to call but the number had been disconnected at the owner's request. After getting this same message for a few days the three of us sent a certified letter to the address to which we had submitted our photos. It came back as undeliverable. Never heard from the producer or anything about the project again.

Nowadays, we certainly would have other avenues by which to track this guy down such as social media, cell phone, text. All we had at our disposal at that time were landline phones and snail mail.

Several years ago I came across an old copy of my audition tape. It got me thinking and I went to social media and searched out the actor who played Mario on "Joanie Loves Chachi." I sent him a private message (back in the day when the platform allowed such messages to just go through), mentioned the project, the mantra and asked if, by any chance, he had even been aware of the project. (I knew what the answer would likely be.) He did reply back saying that he had not heard of the project but was honored that someone would have thought he was a good match to play Papa John as he is friends with his daughter.

Just a Minor Deception

Growing up and even through my adult life, I was not considered particularly attractive. I was not petite, blonde or whatever was the conventional definition at that time or now for that matter.

That being said it closed a lot of acting doors in my not-so-pretty face. But it opened a more unusual one.

It began one year when I showed up to audition for the play "Mary Poppins" that was being put on by a small church theater group. I was about thirteen at the time but looking a bit older, I was just hoping to play one of the housekeepers. I was told that there was nothing for me and sent away. A couple of days later, though, I got a call from someone saying that they knew they had no right to ask me and they would understand if I didn't want to do it but, the little girl whom they had cast as Jane Banks couldn't sing a note. She was horrible. She was cute and looked exactly like what they wanted and her talking voice was perfect. She just couldn't carry a tune. What they wanted from me was for me to stand offstage and sing for her when the singing parts came up.

I agreed, rehearsed with the cast and the night of the show stood offstage and sang "Perfect Nanny" for the little girl who looked the part so well.

This led to other calls for the same "service." Okay, not immediately or even often, but I became the small theater group's answer to Marni Nixon. When I was a sophomore in high school, I did "The Sound of Music" actually singing two roles, Leisl and one of the nuns. A few years later they called upon me to sing for the pretty blonde cast to play Laurie in "Oklahoma!" and demonstrated one of the problems with going this route in a small local theater. Most everyone there knew the lead actress and knew she could not sing. Still I never got mentioned in the program or got to "take a bow." I said at the time that if I ever met Shirley Jones I would have to tell her about this. The responses I got were, "Yeah, like that will happen," and "Even if you do what would she care?" Well, to quote Kris Harmon, "Anything's possible." (Look it up if you want to know.) I recently got to meet Shirley Jones and indeed told her the story which part way through and with a beautiful smile on her face she guessed where it was heading...

that I sang offstage for this person. She was a delight to meet and seemed pleased that I shared my story.

So, back to my original train of thought. The final time I was called to sing offstage was for "The King and I" which holds the irony that Marni Nixon sang for Deborah Kerr in the film version. The actor for that production who played the King coordinated the cast and insisted that I be permitted an introduction with the curtain call. They were apparently told no dice. I said to let it go. But the night of the performance after the cast introduction the actor, still in character as the King silenced the audience and announced, "Ladies and gentlemen, tonight singing for Anna...Michelle Gussow." I was taken aback while being beckoned on stage for the curtain call. The director of the troup was angry, yet there was nothing he could do at that moment. It so happened that I was never called by him to sing again. Maybe it was just a coincidence. Or maybe now that the director had officially been outed he was cornered into actually casting people who could sing.

Don't Cry for Me, Indiana

I am occasionally asked whether I ever actually had a lead role in any stage production or was I always simply relegated to the position of singing offstage.

So... it was 1988 and the casting notice read, "Wanted: Female. Looking specifically for someone who is not ordinarilly considered attractive..." There were some other specifications such as ,had to be a capable singer and so forth' but the main gist was definitely that they were after someone who would not usually be cast in a lead... or as in my case even a secondary role.

That is how I found myself auditioning for the role of Che Guevera for an experimental production of "Evita." And, yes, you read that correctly. The role for which I auditioned and was ultimately cast was that of the guerrilla fighter (or freedom fighter) depending on from which side you view things.

For some who may not be aware in the original incarnation of "Evita" the Che character was supposed to be Che Guevara. I, personally, was unaware until very recently that that has been changed and that "Che" is just some guy.

Anyway, apparently at that time there had been a concept floating around that Che Guevera had really been a female, a fact that was only revealed to her closest allies. The theory goes that it would have been scandalous for the fighters to have been led by a woman so they used the image of her second in command. I do not know from where this originated. It seemed to dissipate quickly, not garnering much acceptance. It is an idea that I do think in today's climate would gain much more traction and likely there would be a new version of "Evita" more closely resembling the stage production in which I performed.

We gave a grand total of one performance. Then the experimental company moved on to their next project... I think it was an all-dog version of "Cats."

A Quickie: One That Got Away

I was once asked if, other than the student films, had I ever completed a project that never went anywhere. The answer to this is, "Yes. Many." The one that really stands out in my mind though, happened in the mid 1980s. I was cast to be the female singing voice for a series of cartoons. The cartoons were shorts like the "Popeye" or "Alvin and the Chipmunks" cartoons. Completed, each ran around five to ten minutes. The working title for the series was "Rock and Roll Aliens." The characters were outer space crime fighters by day and rock and roll stars by night. It turned out that the actress they hired to do the speaking voice for the lead female alien had a dreadful singing voice. Enter the former Marni Nixon of the small church theater group...me, to do vocals. I sang for five episodes, made a few bucks and never heard hide nor hair about it ever again. I admit to having looked on line, never to find any reference whatsoever to anything of that title, or anything even remotely resembling its description.

The Original ACA (Affordable Corporate Actress)

In the 1980s it is likely that I was most well-known for live performance.

They say many things happen by accident and this was truly no exception. It was the summer of 1982 and I had been hired simply to introduce the presenters at a week-long lecture series. As fate would have it the first evening's presenter's plane was late getting in and rather than allowing the attendees to leave their seats, and maybe go into the lobby for coffee, there came the bright idea to have me go out and keep the attendees amused. Talk about having to think fast. I really had no idea what I was going to say or do. I remember stepping out on to the stage and introducing myself. Then, like Baby June in the stage play/movie "Gypsy," to be funny asked, "What's your name?" Everyone laughed. Then I asked ala Paul Dixon, "Where's everybody from?". Then all I could think to do was, like Carol Burnett ask if anyone had any questions. On my honor, someone actually shouted out, "Are those your boobs?"

This is where I learned the number one lesson of posing such an open ended request. Never let them see you taken aback. I responded, "No. I have to get them back to rent-a-center at the end of the week."

I babbled that evening for about twenty minutes. I honestly do not even remember what I talked about but do recall being signaled to wrap it up, and to quickly introduce the lecturer.

Now after that evening oddly enough, all the remaining presenter's seemed to magically end up on late-landing aircraft. I, of course, learned later that these others were in the facility on time and rather than admit that they wanted me to "warm up the group" they continued claiming "flight delay" as the reason for my impromptu story telling. This was the week I officially became know as "that funny woman with the long hair and large chest."

Word spread (as fast as it could without the advent of social media, or even email lists) that there was this person who for a modest fee would amuse the attendees of your corporate training sessions, so I did find myself story telling for several captive audiences. I didn't do what would be considered numerous "shows" but did do enough that I had story requests shouted at me. One of the most requested of my stories I called "Haley's Comet." (If you would like to read it it is in the "Bonus" section of the book.)

The next year the same company asked if I would be open to hosting their talent show. Someone on the board had decided, after watching many talent show episodes of "Laverne and Shirley," that it looked like fun.

I soon found out that hosting the actual show also meant they wanted me to be in charge of the auditions. To anyone who has done this, I likely need not say anything further. You are already groaning in sympathy and wondering how many bottles of aspirin it took me to get through the process.

Through the audition process I learned that every mother had an accordion-playing son who she dreamed would be the next Myron Floren, every male with an electric guitar considered himself the next Jimi Hendrix, and they were all very much mistaken.

That day I sat patiently with two people assigned to be my "committee" listening to dozens of renditions of "Lady of Spain" and just as many performances of "Purple Haze," some less recognizable than others. I only knew what the song was supposed to be because I asked, "What will you be playing for us today?" During the course of the afternoon we also saw amateur magicians, tap dancers and a man who had taken up ventriloquism just days before. (I used this experience in a fan fiction story I wrote about fifteen years ago. An excerpt is in the "Bonus" section of this book.)

One would think that this experience would lead me to decline any future offers to do the same. And one would be wrong. As it turned out my willingness to host outlasted their willingness to continue having the shows. After the first show they asked if I would do it the following year. I did. They asked me again for a third year which I did. They asked me for the fourth year but a month before called to say they were cancelling. Their reason; it was too stressful.

Now somewhere in between talent shows for that company I was getting calls to entertain at other corporate events. I accepted just about all offers as the proverbial "they" weren't exactly beating down my door.

I always thought of myself as an E-lister Eventually, I would be called. But there was a time when I was, for a few the A-lister, the first person to whom they would turn. I became in the corporate world, the person to call when you couldn't afford a real celebrity. I didn't make this up. Apparently, there was a buzz in the corporate midst. It went something like this; "We would really love to have professional entertainment for our company party, but our budget is not going to cover it." "Oh, no problem. Call Michelle. She did our ‚whatever' event and worked within our budget." Yes, I admit I was being called/hired because I was er...um...affordable. God bless Leslie Easterbrook who observed, "You were the celebrity."

In no way am I attempting to make any sort of statement about what other performers did or didn't charge for an appearance. And, had I turned down these offers, the clients were not going to go dig up more funds somewhere to hire the pricier talent. I looked at it this way; I had priced myself into some work. I mean, what was the going rate to have someone that nobody ever heard of, perform at your event?

I did do some pro bono events for charity but, I distinctly remember turning down a performance when I was told they couldn't pay for entertainment because they had spent all the money on liquor.

I usually sang folk songs or other requested numbers if they had someone to accompany me. Sometimes, I would perform with my duet partner Mark Lange with whom I had been singing for several years. He and I usually performed at VA hospitals and the like. However, the most fun I had doing the corporate events was when I performed as a Connie Francis impersonator.

She had been my favorite female singer for some time. I have no idea when I discovered that I could mimic her voice and I actually do not remember how it came up the first time that that was what someone wanted for a performance.

When I did Connie I tended to copy her look from the current time rather than from the 1950s. I was given a makeup job consisting of heavy rouge and lipstick. I was then dressed in what had to be the heaviest sequin gown anyone could get their hands on. It felt like it weighed two tons. There is the part in the song "Where the Boys Are" where Connie always very gracefully raises and lowers both of her arms. In this gown I wasn't sure I could get my arms in the air at all. But somehow I did it. The audience enjoyed the performance and I was invited to give a repeat at the same event the following year.

The third time I did Connie was likely the most memorable. It was part of a show with other impersonators. There was an Elvis, a Bobby Darin, a Frank Sinatra and me. I opened with "Follow the Boys," which I always did to pay tribute to actor Richard Long, one of my all-time favorite actors who had a role in the film of the same name. I segued into "Where the Boys Are," followed by the livelier "Stupid Cupid" and "Lipstick on Your Collar." I closed with "Hava Nagila," which

Connie had included on an album of Jewish favorites. The way she sang it not only made it a "big" number, but was the song I think I sound most like her. To this day I have trouble singing it in my own voice. At the end of the song there is a note that gets held, and the way it is arranged the listener thinks that it's *the* big note, but it goes right into another powerful long-held note with an abrupt finish. To do this and stay in character I was looking up to the ceiling. The audience began to applaud and when I looked back toward them.... they were on their feet! It was my first standing ovation! As of this writing it remains my *only* standing ovation as well. Later that night my fellow performers told me I had really earned it.

Just an added note. I continued to perform with Mark Lange until 1992. Sadly, he passed away in 1993 from leukemia. For those who know me know that I lost my writing mentor in 1980 to the same affliction. I still miss them both terribly.

To Manage or Not to Manage...Oy, What a Question.

In my first humor book "If Two Trains are Traveling in Opposite Directions I Don't Care What the Apples Cost," I have a bit called "Either a Band Manager or a Baby Sitter." I tell about the first time I ever managed a "performer." It was as a favor to the mother of a sixteen-year-old accordion player. (Yes, accordion players seemed to be a common theme in my life.) The young man had been playing, reluctantly, since he was three. His mother. like many who had children who auditioned for those talent shows I mentioned, was convinced that he would be the next Myron Floren. And not surprisingly, his mother was the only one convinced. Everyone else recognized that the young man hated the instrument. It made people less than interested in hiring him for their bar mitzvah parties and whatnot. I did get him into the student film I was in, in which they needed an accordion player for my gypsy-camp number, but after the shoot he threw down the instrument and vowed never to play again. At the same time I vowed I would never manage another performer ever again for as long as I lived.

In that book I jumped from there to more recent history. For this I will share these couple of in-between experiences.

1984 was the first time I was ever asked if I would be interested in managing a group. Even though I had vowed I would not manage again, things were a little slow for me personally and since the situation involved adults who wanted to play rather than a teen who did not, I decided to take the plunge.

The group was called the Flip Flops. They sang mostly covers of songs from the 1960s. The fact that no one ever saw them play was not due to my lack of managerial skill. They broke up two weeks after hiring me because, as the leader put it, "They decided they weren't having any fun with it." I shrugged it off but told myself that I was not going to accept an offer to manage a band ever again.

So it was still 1984 and the bass player from the defunct Flip Flops called, asking if I would be interested in managing the new band he was in. I think they called themselves Gateway to the West. He said they had been practicing for some time and he only contacted me because he was one thousand percent certain they were going to stay a band. I don't really know how I let him, but he got me to agree. I spent the rest of the evening shaking my head and muttering, "Why, oh, why did I say yes?" I called the next day with the intention of backing out, but instead agreed to give them a listen at their next practice session.

Okay, so here's a problem I have to this day. I get a little too excited listening to music that I love. And these guys played oldies, fifties music. At the time that was my favorite. My enthusiasm for the music kept me from making the escape I knew I should have made. This time I got as far as actually booking them to play a pool party and a wedding.

Gateway to the West practiced diligently to ready themselves for the pool party. I had everything and everyone coordinated.

I showed up at the party house. And the band? Well, they were nowhere to be found. They simply never showed up. By the way, my pet peeve to this day is "no shows." After that I contacted the wedding coordinator and unbooked them. Luckily, I had not signed anything with them yet. The band members would not return my calls and "El Lider" even hung up on me. I never did get an explanation and, I was even more emphatic that I would never accept another offer to manage a band ever again.

So, what was it that made me break my number one cardinal rule yet again? Well, Mark had crossed over and the calls from the corporations had stopped. Not mentioning any names here, but one reason was that some of the businesses had gone under. I make no correlation between my entertaining at their events all those years and their subsequent demise. And I was not finding any fresh opportunities in the new location which I lived.

It was 1996 and I was living in Demotte, Indiana. Not exactly your major metropolis, but a far cry from where I had been living just two years prior, a town called Lake Village. There was no lake, although we had a waterfall in the bedroom whenever it rained. And it was hardly big enough to be considered a village. In those many years I had kept my promise to myself about getting involved with local bands. And even though I was living with a musician, and I was helping him wheel and deal for equipment, he personally had not broached the subject. Until....

Said musician got involved with a band called "The Bo' Weevils" featuring "Evil Steve." This band had a huge chance of "getting somewhere." They were all experienced musicians and they had original music. Trouble was they had one member, the lead guitar player, who had one of the biggest egos I'd ever come across. It was so big that he was willing to sacrifice his own success just so the other band members, whom he did not feel worthy of making it, would not have success either. Not only did he have this giant ego, he was also one of the biggest mama's boys I'd ever met. He was the only member of the band that had not wanted me as manager. He wanted his mother. He did not like to rehearse because his mother said he was already good enough and it was the others who needed the practice. He didn't show up on time because he was so important everyone should wait for him. I could go on. Said mother created many issues between the other members too. It seemed I was always running interference and doing damage control. Other times I was tracking down missing band members. The disappearance usually happened before sound check... or tear down. The band eventually broke up and I swore I would never manage another band again... ever.... as long as I lived.

A few years after I moved back to Indianapolis Evil Steve moved there as well, started a band and made his first order of business contacting me. "Babe, even with all the headaches you got us somewhere," he told me. And I was hooked again. I entered the fray on the condition that we have a band meeting so I could make sure there would not be a repeat of the last band. But after a series of members quitting, never having the group rehearsed and ready to go and having to cancel gigs I'd already booked, someone threw in the towel. Maybe it was me. It might even have been Evil. And I said I would never manage another band... ever again... as long as I lived.

While I was writing the book a few years after all this, Steve had put together another group and was again appealing to me to manage. I foolishly agreed. By the time the book came out the whole story contained in its pages about managing Evil Steve's latest band had become obsolete.

Now somewhere in between band managing fiascoes I had started writing and directing my own independent movies. An actor I encountered during the casting process for one of them asked me if I would be interested in managing him. (Don't give me that look. This was not a band.) I had a few lengthy discussions with him about what I expected and signed on to manage him. Thinking it would be prudent to have more than just one actor to promote I asked another actor whom I had auditioned for a project I was writing. This actor was just starting out and was happy to have me take him on.

Managing actors and specifically the one who initially asked me, came with its own set of headaches. This particular actor only wanted lead roles... and not any lead roles, lead, what he called "hottie" roles. And even though he was in his middle thirties he insisted his age range was seventeen to twenty-seven. He also had this idea that he was too big of a star to have to audition. He had a bigger ego than the aforementioned guitar player, which I didn't think possible. He was very difficult and ended up just costing me a lot of money. The second actor gave me a much better experience. He went to the auditions on which I sent him, accepted non-lead roles and actually had a decent amount of success. I considered it a personal success in the managing field when he was cast in a mainstream film called "Desperate Endeavors." He had been cast by its director in another project from an audition I got him. The director liked him so much he wanted to use him in the film. Only real issue I had was he decided to not be an actor any longer.

Things in the local band world shift so rapidly. And dealing with other actors proved to be a pain somewhere. So I made the decision that the only person I would ever manage would be me.

And the Game Changer is...

I think there are some people who don't realize that we did not always have the internet. And, there are some who don't realize that even the entire time we've had the internet we did not have social media platforms. I have been around and doing entertainment in one way or another long before the advent of either and I must tell you from personal experience that both were real game changers.

In the decades in which I started doing the things I have talked about in this book there was no avenue by which to promote oneself. There were a few narrow paths such as putting up flyers, telephone solicitation which I would not do for love or money and the ever popular begging. At the end of performances there was always the plea to, "Please remember to tell your friends and family etc... etc..." Social media changed all that. Now we can beg on line to more people.

Also, back in the day every member of your audience did not arrive equipped with his or her own video capabilities.

Nowadays, every performance has the potential to be videoed from any angle with various sound qualities. Not so in the 1970s and 1980s. Hence, no video documentation of my one and only standing ovation Same even goes for still photographs. If the event did not take pictures ...well, you get the idea. I would give my eye teeth to have pictures of me in the aforementioned two ton sequined gown, heavy rouge and lipstick, posed with my arms out to the sides, leaning ever so slightly with an even slighter tilt of the head. Actually, there was a picture taken of me like that one night. Did they send me a copy? No. Is that picture out there somewhere? Probably. And it's likely labeled "unknown woman as Connie Francis" or even worse "unknown woman in sequined gown."

I have to admit that, in the beginning, I, myself, did not take full advantage of the new technology. I had various websites for my fan fiction writing. I had a website for the Indy Artists' Peace Project and the original Slide Zone Project (now The Migdahlohr Project,) but I still tended to use what I knew. I did a lot of "flyering." So much so I actually had people who knew me from that alone. I also utilized free event calendars in local newspapers. I put the events on the websites, likely because my flyers and other ads directed people to visit the site for more information. And most of the time it slipped my mind to take pictures at the events.

So, in actuality, social media became the *real* game changer. The ability to find and connect with people sharing your interests or old friends and schoolmates indeed changed everything for me. I learned to use the platforms to network and promote like I never had before. It inspired me to take more pictures and even do video promotions.

Now don't get me wrong. I know that using the internet, especially social media, comes with its share of problems. But, using this tool has helped me achieve goals and reach potential I had started to doubt I ever would. Also, because of the continuous feedback I have been encouraged to take more risks. So social media...1, playing it safe...0.

What Part of "No" Didn't You Get?

One of the things I was able to do because of the internet was sign up for on line casting sites. This allowed my headshot and resume to reach more people that it ever had before. What kind of people were clinking on my profiles? Well, that is another story. A story I will tell you now.

I started receiving an inordinate number of emails from producers of adult films. It was the age of open mindedness about these things and no longer a wink, wink to those in the industry. In fact, I learned there were two categories; legitimate porn and illegitimate porn. Everyone was, of course, being warned to do only porn of the legitimate variety.

So, I had and still have a long standing policy of "no nudity." I politely declined all requests for adult film, legitimate or otherwise. I also had to ask any producer, director who contacted me about roles, whether or not they involved nudity of any kind. Of course, I declined to do auditions for any that did.

It was at this time I learned that some people apparently do not understand the definition of nudity. For instance, I was offered a role in a horror film. I made my usual inquiry as to whether or not my role would require nudity. I kid you not, the answer I got back was, "No nudity for your character, except for the scenes where she is topless." He went on to tell me there were a few such scenes. I informed him that that was nudity. He responded that it was not nudity, that it was partial nudity. (Insert eye roll.)

I received another offer via email. This director was more up front and, in fact, proud that he made films that contained nudity. The film he was offering me had a shower scene in which he wanted me to participate. For said scene I was to be paid fifty dollars and, get this...all the beer I could drink. First, as I've mentioned, I do not do nudity. Second, I do not drink alcohol. And I do mean never. I politely declined, expecting that to be the end of it. Instead, I received an email from him asking me why I didn't do nudity. I should have let it go but chose to respond to the message, in effect saying I need not give him a reason. I also asked that he leave me alone.

It seemed to have worked. I did not get another email...until...
The day after they shot their film I actually received an email
from him stating, "We missed you yesterday. We thought
you'd be there." For some reason I answered, reminding him
that I had told him in no uncertain terms that I would not
be. He replied that he had been hoping I would change my
mind. Oy, vey!

Since I am being totally forthright here, I will tell you that
there was one time when I considered baring something
for the sake of the arts. It was for what was, according to
the casting notice, supposed to be a photo shoot depicting
larger natural breasts. It was touted as tasteful, I could bring
someone with me to help me feel more comfortable, and my
submission photo could be clothed as long as it depicted that
I was busty.

Well, talk about misleading! This proved to be one of the
most deceitful casting notices to which I had ever responded.
After submitting my photo (clothed) and resume I got an
immediate response. That in itself was uncommon. It was the
person who had posted the notice thanking me for my photo
and providing more details about the shoot. What he wanted
was...(Okay, I'd better stop here and issue a precaution. If
you have a delicate stomach you may wish to skip the rest of

this paragraph.) What he wanted was to masturbate using my breasts and climax between them. Oh, there still was a photoshoot. He wanted his wife to take pictures of the whole thing. Yikes! He had attached a photo of himself with no shirt telling me it was so I could see that he was "normal." Compared to what? I actually got the feeling he was thinking I would see the picture and find him so appealing that I would jump at the opportunity. I did not even respond to it. I subsequently never trusted another such casting notice.

Interaction is the Best Action

I've always enjoyed doing autograph shows as well as other meet and greet type events. I love interacting with people. It is important to me to make it a pleasant experience for anyone who steps up to my table. It is true that often people approach me with the million dollar question, "Who exactly are you?" And that doesn't bother me. I don't expect that people would know who I am. That's one of the reasons I love to do these events. It is how people will come to learn who I am and hopefully take an interest in my films, music, books, whatever. I enjoy doing events put on by others, but really enjoy staging my own events.

In 2004 I founded The Slide Zone Project. My mission: To bring artists, authors, entertainers from all genres together with the public by hosting local events with no fees for participants nor attendees. Our events include: Individual book signings, Author Fairs, Author Reading Events, Independent Film, Live Variety Shows/Concerts, Meet and Greet events of all kinds. The no fees policy, especially for the presenters, makes for a much more relaxed, enjoyable atmosphere. The pressure of needing to make so many sales to cover the cost of the table is non existent. I continue this mission today under the name The Migdahlohr Project. For the most part anyone who wishes to participate is welcome. I only have one caveat.

In the past decades I have done many meet and greet type events and it never fails that at the event someone will mutter under their breath, "I hate doing these shows." I have never understood why people who don't like to do these things do them and complain rather than decline to participate.

So, the caveat? To participate in a Migdahlohr Project event one must *like* to do this type of event. Trust me on this. People attending the events can tell when the guests do not like being there. It is especially troubling when it is someone that they have wanted to meet for some time. People will be thrilled to step up and meet some one they have never heard of when that author, musician, actor, whomever is pleasant to them and genuinely wants to interact.

Actually, now that I think about it, there is another thing that will get someone uninvited to one of my events. It is if at any time I am asked, "How many (insert item) can I expect to sell?" My events are an opportunity for people to promote themselves to the public. Any sales are a bonus. Maybe there won't be any sales. But, if you are friendly with people and engaging they will remember you, possibly look for you on line, and maybe even buy an item another time.

My future vision for the project is to grow the experience for everyone, hopefully bigger events, most important to me is to reach more people.

In Defense of the NRF

Speaking of meet and greet type events, I must share with you a story I get prompted to share quite frequently. In a room full of people, inevitably, someone will say, "Oh, Michelle, you have to tell that story. You know the one."

So, here is the story they always want to hear.

There is a fan convention in which I participated for several years from about 2003 to 2009. I enjoyed this convention a lot and usually had people approaching my table telling me they had hoped I would be there. Anyway, one year a man came to the table and asked me if he could purchase from the pictures that I had under the table. I looked at him funny, but simply told him I didn't have any pictures other than the ones he could see displayed. He got a very pouty look on his face and whined, "You just don't want to sell them to me."

Now I sincerely had no idea what he was talking about. An author at the table next to me beckoned me with his finger. I leaned closer for him to explain to me that at many fan conventions there are models, even playboy bunnies who have G-rated pictures on display but keep some more adult photos under the table. This relieved me because I was able to turn to the man and honestly say that I didn't have any pictures like those he was seeking. Instead of moving along he repeated that I just didn't want to sell them to him. At that point my neighbor stood up and told the man to move along.

Unfortunately, this was not the end of it. The man returned a few minutes later, again pouting that I had pictures under the table and that I just didn't want to sell them to him. He looked at me pathetically and said, "You don't want to sell them to me because you think I'm ugly." At that point I was really thinking, "If I had such pictures I wouldn't want to sell them to you because you are creeping me out." He finally did give up and walk away."

I related this story to my brother-in-law who decided then and there that I would no longer work convention tables solo. From then on I was to be accompanied by him serving as my official NRF...Nutjob Removal Facilitator.

A Song Still Pounding in my Head

I would be remiss if I did not take a moment to talk about my 2011 short film "Soldier's Song," a film which I wrote, directed and acted in. Filmed in 2009 it did not premiere until two years later. It is a story very personal to me as I knew the man about whom I wrote. He had been in one of the facilities at which Mark Lange and I entertained. The film was made specifically to help draw attention to the overwhelming problem of military suicide. The intention was always to have screenings with discussions following. The film starred Tom Sparx and Scott Ganyo and featuring the most amazing music courtesy of Nick Cappelletti and Moises Bolanos. Nick is also responsible for the very haunting "Death's Lullaby," a song I still have trouble shaking from my brain.

Because of my dedication to using this project to raise awareness of this issue I am including a reading version of the film's script. Though there are some humorous moments in the story please be aware that this is a more serious selection than other offerings in the book.

"SOLDIER SONG"

A Michelle Gussow Film

Tom Sparx Scott Ganyo
Special 10th Anniversary Shooting Script

Fade in: Exterior day. Funeral scene. A RABBI
and CANTOR officiate. (written on screen
will be "Spring 1982") Music starts and
opening titles are over the funeral scene.

Close up on RICK KELLER. Tight shot on eyes.

Flashback. As we dissolve theme music
changes to acoustic guitar, same song.

Dissolve to Interior day. Corner of hospital day room.
VET/GUITAR PLAYER is playing the acoustic music
we are hearing. Camera backs away to reveal all of day
room. RECUPERATING VETS/PATIENTS are seen
playing cards, reading, etc... RICK KELLER sits at one
end of couch reading. There is a cane resting against
the couch beside him. Rick closes his book and rises.
He moves to exit dayroom, passes PATIENT being
wheeled in. Patient is obviously trying to resemble Elvis

Follow Rick down hall to hospital
room. Zoom in on closed door

Cut to: Interior day: Through door reveals all of room.
GREG RAUBINS sits in wheelchair at table in room.
His arms are folded on the table and his head is pillowed

on his arms. There are papers beside his arms. Also on the table are an empty prescription bottle and a glass.

Zoom to Greg's head. Effect of being inside his brain. Ramp up. It slows down:

Interior day: Nursery of a house. Greg at ten years old is sitting in a rocker. MR. RAUBINS gently hands a baby to Greg. There is some interaction. (Let's hope we can get baby to grip Greg's finger)

Greg
You're a little tough guy.
(kisses the baby's forehead)

Ramp up. Slow.

Exterior Day: Greg and DAN ROBBINS are playing one on one football. Dan tackles Greg and the two collapse in a heap, laughing.

Greg
I give. I give.

Ramp up: Slow

Exterior day: Outdoor college graduation ceremony.

Ramp up. Slow

Exterior day: Greg enters an army
reserve recruitment center.

Ramp up: Slow:

Interior day: Bedroom shared by Greg and Dan.

Greg
You know I'm shipping out in the morning.

Dan
War is supposedly over. I still don't
see what they need you for.

Greg
I told you. Government wants us to clean up our
mess. So they're sending in our special unit

Dan
Secret mission or something.

Greg
(laughs)
Something like that

Dan jokingly starts ‚singing' the Mission: Impossible theme song. He stops and grabs Greg in a bear hug. Greg reacts. He kisses the side of Dan's head repeatedly.

Greg
I know. I'm going to miss you too.

ramp up: Slow: Greg and his unit disarming landmines. They are captured.

ramp up: slow On screen says "Fall 1981" Greg and his unit are released. A REP is talking to them.

Rep

...and the government while recognizing everything you have been through in the past years would appreciate it if you would stay and complete the assignment for which you were sent.

ramp up. slow

Cut to: Interior day: Temporary hospital in Vietnam. Greg lying in a bed in a ward type setting. There are other injured soldiers in the ward. Perhaps there are a couple of nurses making rounds. A DOCTOR stands beside the bed.

Greg
What happened?

Doctor
Land mine got ya.

Greg
I can't feel my legs.

Cut to: Exterior day: Military air transport lifts off.

ramp up:

Slow: Interior day: Greg and Rick sit at the table
in the hospital room. They have just completed
a round of the game Mastermind.

Rick
Come on. One more.

Greg
(almost to himself)
Finally get a new roommate I gotta get
one that likes board games.

Rick
It's not a board game. It's a game of cunning and logic.

Greg

It comes in a box. It's a board game.

Rick

There's no board

Greg

(indicating plastic tray)

Then what do you call this plastic thing.

Rick

(has to think a moment)

It's a piece holder.

Greg

(perhaps rolls eyes. Reaches for the instruction
sheet that is on the table and scans it.)

Aha.

(indicates a line)

Says right here ‚place the decoding board..."

Rick

(snatches instructions; feigned indignation)

Well, if you're going to be technical.

Greg

(amused)

It's a board game

Rick

(resigned)

All right. If I admit it's a board game will you play again.

Greg

No. I hate board games. Besides Dr.
Kasden will be here any minute.

Rick

(starts boxing game)

Dr. Kasden?

Greg

She's my shrink. Part of my treatment for the paralysis.

Rick

Does it help.

Greg

If filling out required paperwork helps...

Greg is interrupted by the door opening.
DR. KASDEN enters.

Rick
That her?

Greg
That's her.

Rick is clearly attracted.

Rick
(almost unbelieving)
That's your shrink?

Dr. Kasden
(approaching)
Not all of us look like Bob Newhart. Lt.
Robbins, I see we have a new roommate.

Rick
(rising, extending hand to her)
Lt. Rick Keller.

She does not accept the proffered hand. Somewhat
dejected Rick lets it fall to his side.

Rick
Well, I'm sure I can find something to
do...somewhere. Later, Greg.

He takes his cane and exits the room. Dr. Kasden waits until he leaves to take his vacated seat. She immediately opens her chart. She makes notes throughout the scene

Dr. Kasden
Well, Lt., how are we today.

Greg
I don't know about you but I'm paralyzed. And why does everyone around here always say ,we'?
Dr. Kasden
(attempting a joke)
It's the first thing they teach us in medical school.
(she rights herself)
Still in pain from the waist up.
(Greg nods)
And how do you feel about that?

ramp up. Slow

Interior day: Greg is in bed. DR LANGE stands bedside with chart.

Dr. Lange
That medicine really should be working better. Maybe if we upped the dosage.

Greg

No thanks. Not in to being a zombie.

Dr. Lange

(thinks)

There is another medication I can prescribe. It works differently. Maybe you'll get better results.

ramp up. Slow

Interior day: Greg is sitting in his wheelchair. There is a cassette player... classical music is heard. Greg is expertly conducting.

ramp up. Slow

Interior day: Greg is at the table. Dr. Kasden sits across from him, chart open, making her usual notes.

Dr. Kasden

Still the pain problem. It says here that Dr. Lange changed your medication.

Greg

Yeah, and like the others it worked the first couple of time I took it. Then zip.

(reflecting)

You know it's funny how a person can feel
absolutely nothing in one half of their body
but have nerves on fire in the other half.

Dr. Kasden
So, tell me what you did over the weekend

Greg
(reacting to fact that she chose not to hear him)
I took ballroom dance lessons and went scuba diving.

ramp up. Slow

Interior night: Greg is in bed listening to the
classical music. He is conducting. Rick comes
from the bathroom and moves to his bed.

Rick
I see they changed your meds again.

ramp up. Slow

Interior day: Greg and Rick sit at the table.
There is a chess board set up on the table.

Rick

Now the king can move in any direction but only one
square at a time. Oh, and there's this move called castling.

Greg

How did I let you talk me into this?

Rick

Hey, man, this is more than just a game. It's a commentary
on life. The rulers may think they're all powerful but
really couldn't function without the support of the
other pieces. Lose too many pawns and... check mate!

ramp up. Slow.

Interior day: Greg sits at the table, perhaps with
a magazine. Rick is at his bedside table.

Rick

I know that book is here somewhere. Ah, found it.
(he comes up with the book, approaching table)
Your Dr. Kasden may be hot but, man, she gives
me the creeps. I want out before she breezes in.

(they thump fists {now referred to as
the terrorist thump} Rick exits.

A few seconds pass. The door opens and enters
DR. GILMORE. She has the chart.

Dr. Gilmore
(moving to table)
Lt. Robbins?

Greg
(slightly puzzled)
Yes.

Dr. Gilmore
I'm Dr. Gilmore.

Greg
Where's Dr. Kasden?

Dr. Gilmore
She had a family emergency so the hospital called
my practice and asked me to come talk with you.
(she sits and sets the chart aside and looks intently at Greg)
So, where would you like to begin.
(Greg starts laughing at her)
What's so funny?

Greg
You sure don't know what you're doing. See you're supposed to ask me the questions on that form in there... and only those questions. Proper procedure.

Dr. Gilmore
I see. Well, that's really not my style. So let's say you and I chat and I'll fill out the paperwork later.

Greg
(warning her)
Trouble.

Dr. Gilmore
Hey, I don't work here. What are they going to do to me?
(she gestures with her hands opening the floor to him)

Greg
(joking)
Okay, I'll try it your way.
(a beat)
Wow, I don't know how to start

Dr. Gilmore
Well, what do you do with your time?

Greg

I wank

(she reacts)

Hey, it's the only thing below my waist that still works.

(she reacts)

Actually, you came on a great day. My kid brother Dan
is coming to visit. I've begged for weeks and they're
finally letting someone see me that isn't medical or
military personnel. See I haven't been debriefed yet.

Dr. Gilmore

How long since you've seen him.

Greg

About six months. I have missed him so much. I guess
if I hadn't been injured I still wouldn't be seeing him.

(she is looking at him intently)

God bless shrapnel.

(she reacts)

(we see Dr. Gilmore and Greg talking for a while longer
just to indicate that time passed and their conversation was
lengthier. Perhaps the second conducting piece plays over it)

Greg

I'm afraid our time's up

Dr. Gilmore

I thought I was suppose to say that

Greg

I've actually enjoyed the session.

Dr. Gilmore

(rises)

Me too.

Greg

Don't forget to do the paperwork.

She exits. Greg turns on his cassette player and conducts
Greg looks up. DAN has appeared in the doorway. A
smile spreads across Greg's face. He turns off the music

Greg

(gently)

Hey, tough guy

There is a pause. Dan seems frozen.

Greg

(puzzled that Dan hasn't entered and kissed him)

How about a kiss?

Dan goes to tears, turns like he's looking for a way out. Angle on Greg.

ramp up. Slow

Interior day: Hospital room. Greg and Dan sit at the table in the room. Their right hands are loosely joined resting on the table. Dan is fighting tears. He doesn't face Greg.

Greg

Do they still make those endangered species chocolates?

Dan

(anxious)

Yeah.

Greg

Think you could smuggle some in here next time.

Dan

Sure.

Greg

I'm thinking of retiling the floor with them.

Dan

Okay.

Greg

Dan, look at me.

(Greg reaches up with his free hand and turns Dan's head.)

Talk to me.

(Dan shakes his head)

I know it's hard. It's hard for me. It's also hard for me to see you this upset. Hey, I'm still Greg. Even if I am in this chair.

Dan

It's not that. The paralysis. You're in pain. I can tell.

Greg

Yeah, one of life's ironies. Can't feel a thing from the waist down but the rest of me has nerves that are ablaze.

Dan turns away and tears come.

Greg

(squeezes Dan's hand)

Forget I said that. The important thing is that whatever I'm feeling physically doesn't change how I feel about you. I may not be able to play football with you anymore but I can still love you just as much.

Dan
I just don't want you to hurt.

Greg
I know.

There is an uneasy silence. Dan is experiencing what I like to call emotional claustrophobia.

Dan
(stands suddenly, still holding Greg's hand)
I've got to go.
(stammers)
I'll be back.

Dan starts to let go. But Greg give a slight tug.

Greg
Aren't you forgetting something?

Dan leans in. He hesitates but manages to drop a tentative kiss on Greg's cheek as Greg kisses his cheek in return. Dan pulls back, letting go of his hand.

Dan
I'm sorry.

Dan bolts as we ramp up. Slow.

Interior day: Hospital room. Dr. Kasden sits at the table with Greg. She is making notes in her chart.

Greg
I suppose your not going to ask how
the visit with my brother went.

Dr. Kasden
Oh, did your brother visit?
(to herself)
P.T. check
As Greg is talking Dr. Kasden continues
going down her list checking items.

Greg
(lamenting)
Yes. Yes, he did. And he cried. You know my whole
life I don't think I've ever seen him cry. Even as a
baby, my parents had to guess when he was hungry.
He almost cried the day I shipped out but...
(he stops realizing she's not listening)
Did you check that I went to the
bathroom today all by myself?

Dr. Kasden

Lt., I think the problem here is that
you take these sessions lightly.

Greg

On the contrary, I take these sessions very seriously.
It's YOU I take lightly. You know what. You're
always asking me stuff. How about I ask a question.
How come nobody ever talks about the war? I mean
most of us here came by way of the Westmoreland
Express. Yet no one ever talks about it.

Dr. Kasden

The administration feels it's not conducive
to your healing process.

Greg

Oh, really. Well, it sure as hell was conducive to our
injury process. And it's not just us. It's our families...

Dr. Kasden

Counseling is made available to....

Greg

Yeah, we know all about the so called
therapy for military families.

(to himself)
It's about as good as this.

Dr. Kasden
(back to her chart)

Dietary says you didn't eat your breakfast this morning.

Greg
Oh, yeah, that's earth shattering in
the scheme of my recovery.

Dr. Kasden
Well, proper nutrition is...

Greg
I know conducive to my healing process.

Fast motion blur. Slow.

Interior day: Greg is in bed. Dr Lange is
bedside. Greg is visibly in pain.

Dr. Lange
You might feel better if you got out of bed.

Greg
And I might not. Look can't I just be in pain in peace.

Dr. Lange
I put in for a stronger...
(he stops. Greg is shaking his head)
What?

Greg
Nothing. You wouldn't get it anyway.

Dr. Lange
(writing on chart)
I'm putting in an order for you to dispense your own
medication. Since you were going to transition soon
anyway. That way it can be as needed. Not to exceed
four doses in an hour period. Perhaps it will help
for you to have more control over the situation.
(he closes chart)
I'll...

Both
See you tomorrow

ramp up: Slow: Interior day: Hospital room. Greg is
in his wheelchair by the bed. Dan sits on the bed.

Dan
(near tears as usual)
I wish there was something I could do.

Greg
You are. Just being here.

Dan
But it's obvious the pain is getting worse.

Greg
(trying to joke)
At least the paralysis isn't. Okay, not funny.
I do get to dispense my own pills.

Dan is reacting silently.

Greg
(coaxing, tugs Dan's arm)
You know when you were little and got upset
all I had to do was hold you in my lap.
(he manages to pull Dan onto his
legs. Dan tries to pull away)
It's okay. I don't feel a thing.

Dan breaks down. Greg holds him close.

Cut to: Interior night: Greg is in bed. The cassette
player is on but this time it is not classical music.
It is of a darker nature. Rick enters the room
with book in hand. He reacts to the music.

Rick

(moving to own bed)

Oh, man, what is that?

Greg

(turns down volume)

It's called "Death's Lullaby"

Rick

(almost to himself)

And with good reason.

Rick sets his book aside and removes his robe. As he gets into bed Greg raises the volume on the boombox.

Rick

(listens for a moment; to himself obviously contemplating hearing it all night, deadpan)

Great.

(a beat)

Man, what happened to that (imitates Beethoven's Fifth) you usually listen to?

Greg

Not in the mood. When they brought the media cart around I told them I wanted something darker.

Rick

Well....you got it.

Greg

(out of nowhere)

Rick, you got a brother.

Rick

I've got a sister.

Greg

Not the same. I can't explain it but it's not the same.

Rick

Man, you're a little weird sometimes.
Did I ever mention that?

Greg

All the time. You know I never tell Dan how
much pain I'm actually in. He just knows. And
that hurts him... a lot. The fact that he's hurting.
Well, that hurts me. It's a vicious cycle.

Rick

You should talk to your shrink about that.

Greg

I would but it's not on her chart. I wish I
could talk with Dr. Gilmore again.

Rick

(climbing into bed)
She's not the looker Dr. Kasden is.

Greg

Maybe. But Dr. Kasden's not the human being she is.

Greg cranks the volume on the CD player. Rick folds
the pillow around his ears and turns away from Greg.

Fast motion blur: Slow:

Interior day: Hospital room: Greg sits at the table. The
cassette player is on a chair beside him. He is listening
to the dark music. Rick emerges from the bathroom. He
heads to the cassette player and hits the pause button.

Greg

I was listening to that.

Rick

You've been listening to that song for hours. It's
getting to me. I'm starting to hear it in my sleep.

(he moves to his bed and retrieves his book)

Greg

Sorry, this thing didn't come with headphones.

Rick

Not a problem. I'm going to the day room.
(he starts out, turns back and hits the button to unpause)

Rick exits the room bumping into Dr. Kasden on his
way out. She glares in his direction a moment then
enters to take her usual seat. She turns off the boombox,
sits, flips open the chart and poises herself to write.

Dr. Kasden

So, how did we sleep last night?

Greg

We didn't. Well, maybe you did. My mind is too cluttered.
I know you're not going to ask about that because it's
not on that form you have to fill out but I'm going to
tell you anyway. It's cluttered because I'm hurting....

Dr. Kasden

You're in charge of your own medication now

Greg

Not that kind of hurting. Well, that too. But, my
brother will be here later and I'm not sure I want
him here. It hurts him too much to see me in pain.
It breaks my heart. I want to see him but I don't

Dr. Kasden is searching her chart as if
wondering where to put this information.

Greg

Of course, you're on pins and needles to ask why I refused
to eat the undercooked cream of wheat this morning.
(a beat) It's because I prefer the overcooked oatmeal.

She is actually noting this.

Greg

(reaches out, grabs her pen and tosses it across the room)
Will you stop filling out forms for five seconds and
listen to me. The whole time I've been here I've endured
not only the pain and paralysis but the bullshit system.
Well, I've had it. I'm sick of them sticking me in places
I can't feel anything and asking me if I feel it. I'm
fed up with them coming in everyday asking me to
rate my pain on a scale from one to ten. It hurts! And
I've certainly had enough of this so called therapy

Dr. Kasden is fidgeting as if she doesn't
know what to do without her pen.

Greg
(calming)
Look, I don't want to do this today. Find your pen
and write in your little chart that I was uncooperative.
That should cover your ass. Just leave. Please

Dr. Kasden
(rises)
I'll...

Greg
(finishes her sentence)
see you tomorrow.

She glances about the floor

Greg
(gestures)
It's over there.

Dr. Kasden retrieves her pen.

Dr. Kasden
Don't forget to take your medicine.
(she exits)

Greg
How could I?

Greg wheels to his bedside cabinet. He takes a pill
bottle from the top of the cabinet and places it in his
lap. He opens a drawer and retrieves paper and a pen.
He closes the drawer and returns to the table. He sets
the paper and pen on the table. He takes the pill bottle
from his lap, studies it and puts it on the table. He turns
on the TV but cuts the sound and perhaps opts again
for the CD he has been listening to. He opens the pill
bottle and dispenses one tablet, swallowing it without
the benefit of water even though there is a glass and
pitcher on the table. He starts to write something.

Greg
(to himself to see how it sounds)
Dan, no offense, tough guy, but I'd
rather you not see me today...

(he stops, crumples the paper and tosses it. He thinks for a
moment then again reaches for his pill bottle. This time he
downs its entire contents, using the water. He starts to write
and continues until the he feels the first effects of the pills.
He quickly finishes the letter, takes another sheet of paper

and writes a few sentences. The drugs overtake him. He rests his arms on the table and pillows his head on them.

ramp up ends with bright white light

Exit Greg's brain.

Interior day: Back to the present. Rick enters the room.

Rick
(talking as he enters)
Hey, man, this should make you laugh or at least chuckle. There's this new guy...thinks he's Elvis, just ,cause he has black hair. He never says anything without adding ,thank you, thank you very much'

It all of a sudden dawns on him that Greg is not awake. He turns off the cassette player then notices the note. He picks it up and reads.

Greg's voice
Please give this letter to my brother and you can tell the doctor I finally figured out what to do with the pills to get them to work.

Rick feels for a pulse in Greg's neck.

Rick

Damn!

Cut to: Interior day. Hallway. Two orderlies wheel
gurney with body out of hospital room. Rick follows
out of the room. Dan approaches, makes a realization
and goes to tears. Rick steps up and holds him.

Dissolve to: Interior day. Day room. The body being
wheeled passed the open door catches attention of
the men. Perhaps it is from the squeak of the gurney.
Rick and Dan follow. We hear the guitar player
continuing his music. Close up of Rick and Dan

Dissolve: Exterior day: End of funeral. Close
up of Rick and Dan. Move back. People file
passed them shaking their hands etc..

Abrupt cut to black. Music is heard again
and goes into ending theme.

No, It's Not Mid-Life Crisis

When referring to certain viewpoints I hold on things I find myself saying, "I didn't just wake up one day and decide I would think such and such." But I literally woke up one morning with the idea to promote myself as a pin-up girl. Yes, you heard me right. A pin-up girl. Now I am not talking about something that one would have to hide in a brown paper wrapper. My concept involved the 1950s' style pin-up girl. This is to whom I decided to pay homage.

Okay, maybe I really didn't wake up one morning with the idea. What I woke up with was the decision to go ahead and do it. It was an idea that had been floating around in the back of my mind for a while. it was an idea that evolved from the fact that on social media no matter what poignant post I made it never gotten the reactions or comments that I got when I posted a new publicity picture.

So, at age fifty-five I decided to promote myself as "Your Pin-up Girl/" I did what I always do when I begin any new endeavor. I created a social media page and invited those who had reacted so strongly to the photos I had shared over the years, to like the page. It does keep me on my toes as far as having up-to-date pictures. I make a new cover picture for the month and do my best to rotate the profile pictures. I have had a lot of fun with it. I am even going to turn a couple of my new photos into posters.

Fancy that. The little girl who wasn't considered cute enough to be the tightrope walker in the circus, the teen girl, young adult who was told she was not pretty enough and was relegated to singing offstage for the pretty leads who couldn't, the woman who was once told she was nothing to write home about is now "Your Pin-up Girl."

FUN FACTS AND
INTERESTING INFORMATION

When I was a very little girl, any time I put on a pair of sunglasses my mother told me I looked like a movie star. (Yes, ironic considering she really didn't want me to be one.)

When I was about nine-years-old I created a sitcom, on paper anyway. I wrote a few episodes worth of scripts. The series was called "Martha and Me" and it resembled a female version of "Leave it to Beaver," if it had been from the point of view of Larry Mondello. Even though I am now quite familiar with "Leave it to Beaver," at that point in time I had never seen the show.

Though I have many actors that I really love, my all time favorite actor is Pete Duel, best known as Hannibal Heyes in the TV series "Alias: Smith and Jones."

As an author I get asked quite frequently who *my* favorite author is. Honestly, I do not really have one. When it comes to reading material I prefer biographies/autobiographies to anything else. My favorite biographical story is "Shot in the Heart." Its author is a man named Mikal Gilmore.

I've gone through many "favorite singers" in my lifetime. For the last three years it has been Rick Nelson.

As a singer I have frequently been asked with whom would I most like to duet. I had even been asked this in front of my duet partner at that time. The answer to that was and still is Jimmy Demers.

Even though I've never been asked, for decades I have had a running list of actors with whom I would like to work. Sadly, over the years I have had to cross off names as they have crossed over. Some of those with whom I wanted to work and cannot because they have crossed over are: Richard Long, Sal Mineo, Paul Regina, Eric Douglass, Richard Hatch and James Stacy. I still hope to work with Drake Hogestyn, Martin Landau, Ben Murphy (although he is retired) Martin Sheen, and Julian Stone.

I always thought it would be funny to be recognized for something totally unexpected like someone saying "Weren't you Marcia in the play about Masada?" Occasionally, I got recognized by people at whose companies events I had played. When I had the column in the Jewish Post and Opinion I got recognized a few times. I even experienced a woman getting totally excited about seeing me. It was at a baby naming party. I had prepared the desserts. She and her husband entered and she literally freaked out, having an "It's her!" moment. She apparently enjoyed my column that much.

That being said. I had a column in the "Jewish Post and Opinion" for a while. Those columns were the basis for my first humor book.

When I was twelve-years-old I got to be kissed by Peter Lupus of "Mission: Impossible" fame. It was on a local March of Dimes telethon. Can I count that as my first on-screen kiss? For real, it was my first kiss of any kind. It was also my very first time on television, although, I was far too starstruck and nervous to appreciate it.

During the late 1980s the song "Bashana Haba'ah" was considered my theme song.

I did background work on the movie "Stranger than Fiction" starring Will Ferrell.

I still can be seen doing student films. I do them mostly to be of help.

Look for me on Lec Zorn's show "Super Deep Movie Analysis." I co-analyze all the movies in the "Rocky" series with him.

In 2018 I had a role in an episode of "True Firsts" about Moses Fleetwood Walker. I learned upon arrival to the set that I was to play the role of a racist. It turned my stomach but I believe one should not sugar coat racism. And it was important to the project to show the "ugly" in telling this man's story. I will tell a little secret: the director said I needed to be very angry with this man. To get into that frame of mind I told myself I had seen him kick a puppy.

This book you are holding is my fourth, and is the second to be humor. The other two are dessert recipe books.

Many people know me for my participation in a deconstructed sketch comedy. There are several videos and I portray different characters, all with different makeup and/or wigs. Most people have said they did not know it was me when the character was in a wig. To find these go to youtube and check out Brothers Kissing Productions

I am the host of an interview/talk show on youtube called "On the Couch with Michelle Gussow. It can be found by searching its title or visiting the Irrespressible Productions channel.

BONUS BITS

A Taste of Notariety

I had an odd experience in 1989 when I was in Los Angeles. At the hotel at which I was staying one of the desk clerks said, "Didn't I see you in a movie?" I admit my first thought was that this was a come-on line. I said, "I don't think so." When he insisted, I laughed slightly and told him he must be mistaken. He persisted, "It was you. You were singing in a gypsy camp." I still didn't admit it but I knew that somehow he had to have actually seen me in "Runner Astray" I mean, one just doesn't pull ‚singing in a gypsy camp' out of thin air. During the few months I was in L.A. two more people approached me, stating the same thing, that they had seen me in a movie and I had been singing in a gypsy camp. Somehow a copy of that film existed other than the one turned in as the film assignment, the one that was never to be returned and now belonged to the school... To this day I cannot say for certain where these young men had seen the film.

Haley's Comet

If they gave a prize for going through junior high and high school without having even one date...well, that would have been the award I would have won. I was even voted girl most likely to never get asked out. This is why when the opportunity actually arose I said, "Yes."

It was in the spring of my freshman year of college and the young man to whom I said, "Yes" was what they affectionately called a "cutter." (I will call him Brad.) He was someone who lived in the college town but did not attend the university. (You might be familiar with this term from the movie "Breaking Away.") He wasn't bad looking, just quirkier than most...even by my standards. But I accepted his invite to see a movie because me getting a date was as rare as the appearance of Haley's Comet. I don't remember which movie we were going to see. I only remember it was not the one at which we ended up.

So, now came the day of the date. The young man knocked on my dorm room door. Opening it I discovered he was accompanied by a young boy. Nowadays the immediate reaction would be, "Oh, dear heavens he had a kid." Common sense at the time told me this was likely a little brother.

Brad greeted me enthusiastically...maybe a little too enthusiastically and then added as though there was nothing unual about his being there, "This is my little brother Joey."

I must pause here for just a second to tell you what went through my mind at that moment of introduction "Of course it is. They're all named Joey. It seemed for some reason for the past decade every little brother I ever met was named Joey."

Now back to the story. Brad continued, "So, are you ready?"

"Are we dropping him off at a friend's house or something?" I asked.

Brad seemed confused by my question. "No," he responded as if he couldn't understand why I had asked. "He's coming to the movie with us."

We all remember that episode of the classic sitcom "The Brady Bunch" where Greg and Bobby had the bet that Greg wouldn't be able to do twice as many chin-ups and the loser had to do whatever the winner said for an entire week. Bobby won the bet and ended up making Greg take him on his date to a drive-in movie. So my first thought was that maybe this guy lost some kind of bet in a sinilar scenario. But, no, apparently Joey had said he wanted to go and Brad revealed that he never denied the kid anything.

Okay, so right then and there I should have declined to go and told him if he wanted to spend the afternoon with his brother then he was free to do so... but..Haley's Comet. Who knew when I would ever be asked out again? I wanted to say that I had at least been on one date, no matter how miserable, so I surrendered.

I spend the next couple of hours in a movie theater watching some movie that Joey wanted to see and watching Brad jump up every fifteen minutes to get something from the concession counter. I came to the conclusion that no date at all would have been more fun that this. I was relieved when it ended and I was finally driven to the entrance to my dorm building. As I was emerging from the car Brad asked, "So what are the three of us going to do next weekend?" Uh, no. Maybe when Haley's Comet comes around again.

Excerpt from my Fan Fiction Story "Talent Show"

Note: I have altered the names for this publication

"Here's the aspirin you wanted." Mike dropped two tablets into his wife's waiting hand. He handed her a can of ginger ale to wash them down. Michelle swallowed the pills. But the performance of the auditioning accordion player was destined to counteract the effect of the medicine.

Mike gave Michelle's shoulder a sympathetic pat. She looked to him and smiled her appreciation. She glanced to the young man on stage. "Why is it that everybody whose mother forced them into music lessons thinks that they are the *only* ones who can play "Lady of Spain?" This was already the fifth rendition the committee had heard and the day was not even half over.

For Michelle, Liz and JoAnne the day had started out at 7:00 a.m. It was time for the annual talent show for fire fighters and their families. Michelle had to hold auditions and Liz and JoAnne offered to assist with the fiasco. It was amazing the "talent" that came out of the woodwork for these events.

"I still think that you and Mike should emcee the show," Liz said over the crash of the young man trying to case his instrument. "You two were hysterical as Sonny and Cher last year."

"I hired someone to emcee this year," she responded.

Paula arrived on the scene. She handed Michelle an invoice. "Here's the bill for the flyers. What did I miss?"

Mike sat on the table. "Five accordion players, four tap dancers, three magicians, two headaches..."

"And a partridge in a pear tree," Michelle sang sarcastically.

Dessert Break

Both of my dessert recipe books included some humor, so I find it only fitting that my humor book include a little dessert.

Supernaturally Sweet Surprise Cake

1 Box French Vanilla Cake Mix
Ingredients needed to prepare cake mix
Frosted oat cereal with marshmallows
4 tbsp. butter or margarine, melted
1 tbsp. brown sugar, optional
1 tsp. ground cinnamon, optional
1 Tub classic white ready to spread frosting.

Separate the cereal from the marshmallows. Set aside the marshmallows. For this recipe you will need 1 cup of coarse crumbs made from the cereal. You will not use all of the cereal. (I put my leftover cereal in a bag with a zipper closure and keep it stored with my other baking ingredients.)

Combine the cereal crumbs with the butter or margarine. Add brown sugar if you think you would like it to be sweeter. Add cinnamon, if desired. Set the mixture aside.

Preheat oven according to directions on the cake mix package. Prepare batter according to directions. Spray a bundt pan with cooking spray or grease and flour the pan. Pour half of the batter into the prepared pan. Cover the batter with the prepared cereal crumb mixture. Pour the remaining batter over the top. Bake as directed. Cool completely. Frost with the white icing. Use the reserved marshmallows to decorate the cake. Use as many or as few as you like. Enjoy!

Afterword

I had always said that the E-list meant that eventually I'll get called. I haven't waited on anyone to call me for some time. I've jumped into the deep end and just work to make things happen. I guess I am still an E-lister, Eventually more people will know who I am and experience the books I write, watch films I make, tune into the interview show and attend the events I stage. But it's all good. I am blessed to be doing what I love and helping others do what they love.

Here is to everyone finding their passion, creating inner peace, and living their dreams.

About the Author

Long time resident of Indianapolis, Michelle Gussow is an independent film writer, director and actor. She is also a folk singer and public speaker. She can be seen in her own talk/ interview show "On the Couch with Michelle Gussow" as well as at a meet and greet near you.

Printed in the United States
By Bookmasters